EVERYTHING IS CONNECTED

REIMAGINING THE WORLD ONE POSTCARD AT A TIME

KERI SMITH

D0522749

Particular Books

PARTICULAR BOOKS

Published by the Penguin Group
Penguin Books Ltd, 80 Strand, London WC2R 0RL, England • Penguin Group (USA) Inc., 375 Hudson Street, New York, New York 10014, USA • Penguin Group (Canada), 90 Eglinton Avenue East, Suite 700, Toronto, Ontario, Canada M4P 2Y3 (a division of Pearson Penguin Canada Inc.) • Penguin Ireland, 25 St Stephen's Green, Dublin 2, Ireland (a division of Penguin Books Ltd) • Penguin Group (Australia), 707 Collins Street, Melbourne, Victoria 3008, Australia (a division of Pearson Australia Group Pty Ltd) • Penguin Books India Pvt Ltd, 11 Community Centre, Panchsheel Park, New Delhi – 110 017, India • Penguin Group (NZ), 67 Apollo Drive, Rosedale, Auckland 0632, New Zealand (a division of Pearson New Zealand Ltd) • Penguin Books (South Africa) (Pty) Ltd, Block D, Rosebank Office Park, 181 Jan Smuts Avenue, Parktown North, Gauteng 2193, South Africa

Penguin Books Ltd, Registered Offices: 80 Strand, London WC2R 0RL, England

www.penguin.co.uk

First published in the United States of America by Perigee Books, an imprint of Penguin Books (USA) Inc., 2013

First published in Great Britain by Particular Books 2013
001

Copyright © Keri Smith, 2013

Art and design by Keri Smith

The moral right of the author has been asserted

Printed in China

A CIP catalogue record for this book is available from the British Library

ISBN: 978-0-141-97744-7

DOCUMENT Things YOU **SEE** ON YOUR way to **Mail** this POSTCARD.

PLACE
STAMP
HERE

THIS CARD SEEMS TO BE ASKING YOU TO TAKE A
JOURNEY OF SORTS. YOU WILL USE IT TO EXPLORE
THE WORLD VIA AIMLESS WANDERING.
- ROLL THE DIE.
- TAKE FIVE STEPS IN THE DIRECTION INDICATED.
- CONTINUE ROLLING THE DIE. DOCUMENT YOUR
  MOVEMENT.

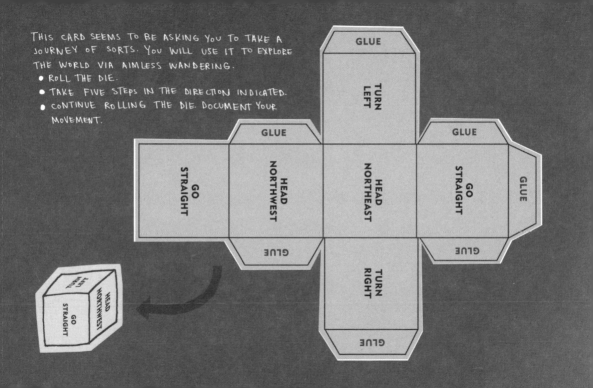

PLACE
STAMP
HERE

DROP A COIN OR A ROCK ONTO THIS CARD.
FOLLOW INSTRUCTIONS.

Plate 46

Random Experience Generator

Leave this postcard in a public place.	Send this to someone you haven't seen in a long time.	Write a letter using a pseudonym.
Write a letter that only makes sense to the recipient.	Write a letter using no "E's."	Write a letter about what you did today.
Send this postcard to a former teacher.	Leave this postcard in a tree.	Write a letter giving the recipient a challenging task.
Send this postcard to someone in your best friend's family.	Write a letter using your wrong hand.	Send this postcard to a foreign country.

PLACE
STAMP
HERE

YOU HAVE IMMENSE POWERS.
REPURPOSE THIS EMPTY LOT.
TRANSFORM IT INTO SOMETHING
THAT WILL HELP THE PLANET.

PLACE
STAMP
HERE

INCONVENIENCE

TAKE THIS POSTCARD
EVERYWHERE YOU GO FOR
ONE WEEK. YOU MUST
PLACE IT IN FULL VIEW
AT ALL TIMES.

PLACE
STAMP
HERE

SECRET IDENTITY PROFILE
(WHO WOULD YOU LIKE TO BE?)

NAME:
PLACE OF BIRTH:
DATE OF BIRTH:
PROFESSION:
LIKES:

DISLIKES:

LOCATION:

LIFESTYLE SYNOPSIS (DAILY ACTIVITIES):

PERSONAL HABITS:

HOBBIES:

GROUPS & ASSOCIATIONS:

SOCIAL LIFE:

PLACE
STAMP
HERE

DEAR FRIEND,

THIS IS A CHAIN LETTER.
IT'S ONLY PURPOSE IS TO SEE
HOW FAR IT CAN GO.
ADD YOUR NAME AND LOCATION
TO THE BOTTOM OF THE LIST.
THEN SEND THE LETTER TO
ONE FRIEND.

ORIGINATOR: _

_ _

_ _

_ _

_ _

_ _

PLACE
STAMP
HERE

THIS IS YOUR VERY OWN PLANET.
YOU MUST ADD THINGS TO IT TO MAKE
IT FLOURISH.
- CREATE A LEGEND WITH SYMBOLS
  TO ADD BUILDINGS, PEOPLE, AND THINGS
  FROM YOUR IMAGINATION.
- DESCRIBE THE WEATHER AND THE INHABITANTS;
  ADD ROADS, ETC.

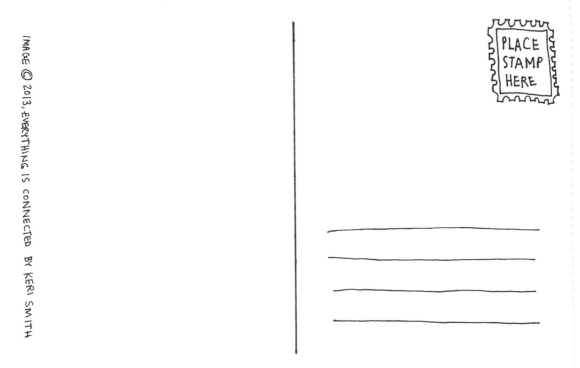

PLACE
STAMP
HERE

ITINERARY.

- GO TO THE CLOSEST PARK.

- SPEND 10 MINUTES LOOKING AT THE SKY. WHAT DO YOU SEE?

- DOCUMENT YOURSELF STANDING UNDER A TREE (PHOTO, DRAWING, ETC.).

- ARRANGE SOMETHING YOU FIND INTO A CIRCLE (LEAVES, STONES, ETC.).

- LIST THE NUMBER OF PEOPLE YOU SEE.

- LEAVE SOMETHING OF YOURS IN A SECRET LOCATION.

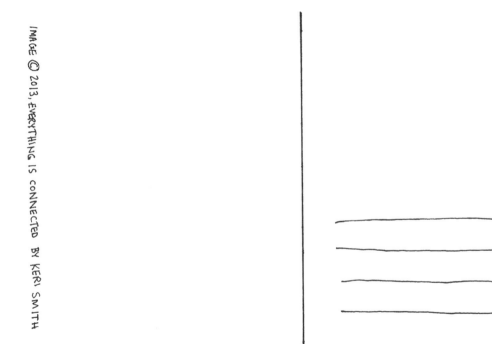

PLACE
STAMP
HERE

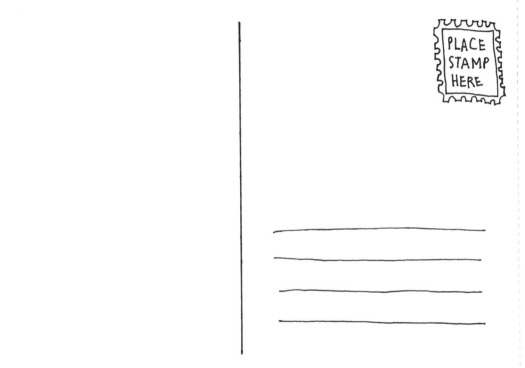

PLACE
STAMP
HERE

THIS IS A PORTABLE HOLE/PORTAL.

MAKES THINGS DISAPPEAR AT WILL.

- CUT OUT.
- AFFIX THE HOLE TO ANY SURFACE.
- USE.

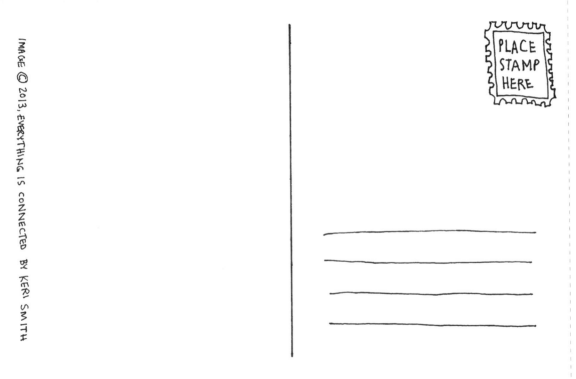

PLACE
STAMP
HERE

CARVE SOMETHING ONTO THIS TREE.

PLACE
STAMP
HERE

THIS
POSTCARD
IS A
SCULPTURE

USE THIS CARD TO CREATE A
THREE-DIMENSIONAL OBJECT.
EXHIBIT IT SOMEWHERE.

PLACE
STAMP
HERE

THIS IS A
PUBLIC SPACE.
INVITE PEOPLE TO ADD SOMETHING
TO THIS PAGE.

PLACE
STAMP
HERE

DO NOT STICK ANYTHING HERE. DO NOT SCRIBBLE ON THIS POSTCARD. DO NOT COVER UP THIS TYPE. DO NOT TOUCH THIS POSTCARD WITH DIRTY HANDS. DO NOT READ THIS POSTCARD WHILE EATING. DO NOT WALK ON THIS POSTCARD WITH YOUR SHOES. DO NOT RUB THIS POSTCARD WITH DIRT. DO NOT FOLD DOWN THE CORNERS OF THIS POSTCARD. DO NOT WRITE NOTES TO YOUR FRIENDS HERE. DO NOT TEAR THIS POSTCARD. DO NOT GET THIS POSTCARD WET. DO NOT LET A FRIEND WRITE ON THIS POSTCARD. DO NOT TRY TO COVER UP THIS POSTCARD. BREAK THE RULES.

PLACE
STAMP
HERE

Mess up this shirt.

Some ideas:
• Crack an egg, wipe it off.
• Splatter something.
• Drip ink. Doodle.

PLACE
STAMP
HERE

Create a mess here with a friend while having lunch together.

PLACE
STAMP
HERE

HIDE THIS POSTCARD
IN YOUR NEIGHBOR'S
YARD.

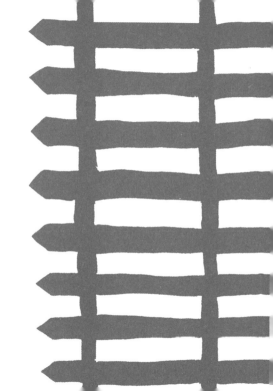

PLACE
STAMP
HERE

COLLECT FRUIT STICKERS HERE.

PLACE
STAMP
HERE

CONVERSATION STARTER BADGE

1. CUT ALONG DOTTED LINE.
2. AFFIX TO CLOTHING.

PLACE
STAMP
HERE

PLACE
STAMP
HERE

COUPONS

THIS COUPON ENTITLES
THE USER TO DO THE
OPPOSITE OF WHAT
S/HE PLANNED FOR THE
DAY.

THIS COUPON ENTITLES
THE USER TO TURN
THEIR WORLD INTO AN
IMAGINED REALITY FOR
A FEW HOURS.

THIS COUPON ENTITLES
THE USER TO MOVE AS
SLOWLY AS POSSIBLE
WHILE GOING ABOUT THEIR
EVERYDAY ACTIVITIES.

THIS COUPON ENTITLES
THE USER TO SOME
DEEP BREATHS.

THIS COUPON ENTITLES
THE USER TO ONE DAY
TO DO SOME RANDOM
WANDERING.

THIS COUPON ENTITLES
THE USER TO DO
SOMETHING COMPLETELY
OUT OF CHARACTER.

THIS COUPON ENTITLES
THE USER TO WEAR
A DISGUISE.

THIS COUPON ENTITLES
THE USER TO
A DIFFERENT
PERSPECTIVE.

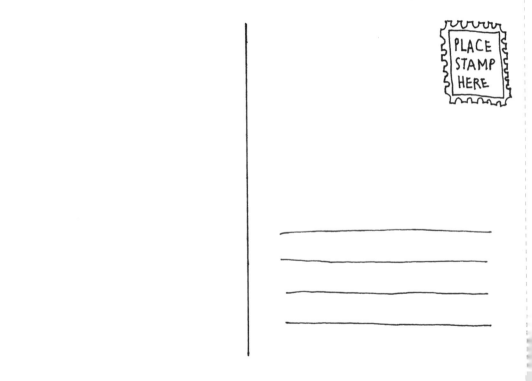

PLACE
STAMP
HERE

SEE HOW MANY TIMES YOU CAN MAIL THIS POSTCARD BACK AND FORTH TO A FRIEND.

WRITE VERY SMALL SO YOU CAN ADD TO IT EACH TIME.

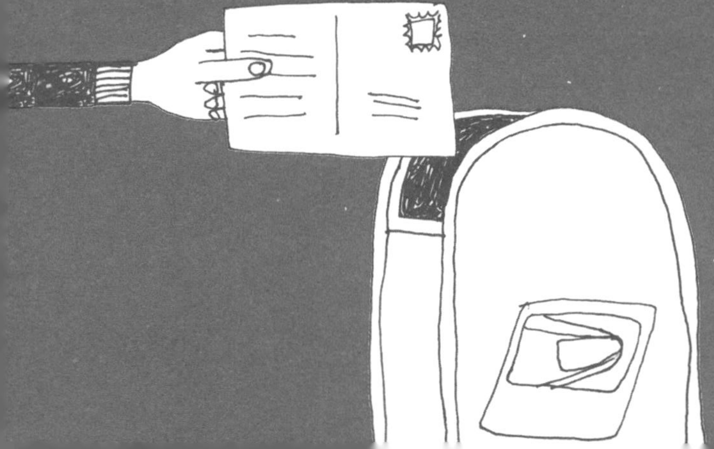

PLACE
STAMP
HERE

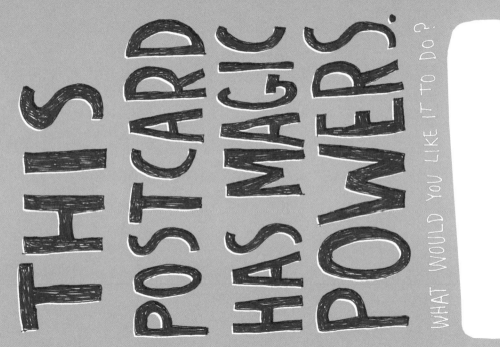

THIS POSTCARD HAS MAGIC POWERS.

WHAT WOULD YOU LIKE IT TO DO?

PLACE
STAMP
HERE

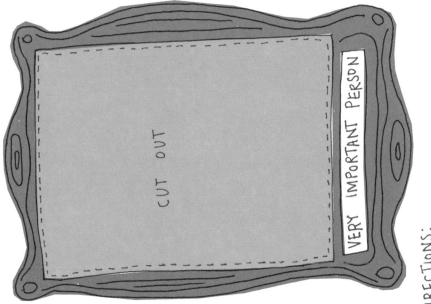

CUT OUT

CUT OUT

VERY IMPORTANT PERSON

DIRECTIONS:
- CUT OUT SQUARE.
- HOLD UP FRAME AND PHOTOGRAPH PEOPLE.
- SEND THEM A COPY.

PLACE
STAMP
HERE

USE THIS SPACE

TO WRITE SOMETHING REALLY
IMPORTANT AND SECRET
(SOMETHING YOU'VE NEVER TOLD
ANYONE ELSE). CHOOSE ONE
OF THE FOLLOWING OPTIONS:

- DESTROY THE CARD BEFORE
  ANYONE SEES IT.

- MAIL IT TO A STRANGER.

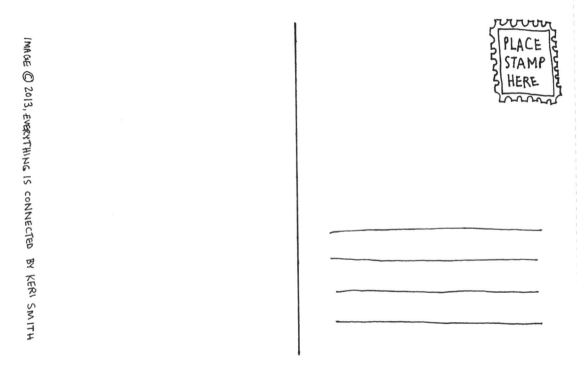

PLACE
STAMP
HERE

I THINK WE SHOULD MEET IN PERSON, INSTEAD OF CONNECTING ON facebook.

DATE:
TIME:

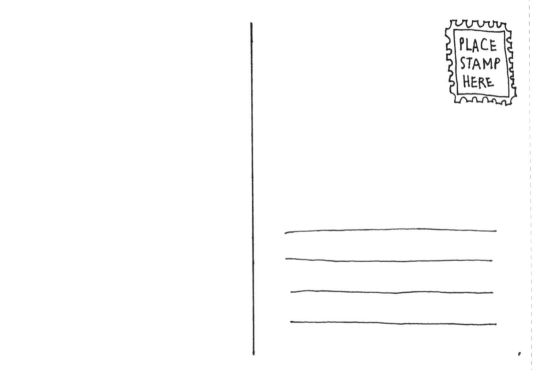

PLACE STAMP HERE

DO SOMETHING INTERESTING WITH **THESE** HOLES.

PLACE
STAMP
HERE

THIS IS A PORTRAIT OF
ME AS A SUPERHERO.

THIS IS A PORTRAIT
OF YOU AS A BAD GUY.

PLACE
STAMP
HERE

THIS IS A GAME.

PLAYERS TAKE TURNS PLACING THIS POSTCARD
IN A DIFFERENT LOCATION FOR EACH ROUND.

THERE ARE FIVE ROUNDS. IN EACH ROUND
PLAYERS TAKE TURNS RETRIEVING THIS POSTCARD
ACCORDING TO THE REQUIREMENTS ON THE LIST.

OPTIONAL: TIME EACH ROUND. GIVE EACH PLAYER
TWO MINUTES.

CREATE FIVE MORE REQUIREMENTS (ROUNDS).

ROUND ONE: RETRIEVE THIS POSTCARD
WITH EYES SHUT.

ROUND TWO: RETRIEVE THIS POSTCARD
WITH NO HANDS.

ROUND THREE: CONVINCE A THIRD PARTY TO
RETRIEVE THIS POSTCARD
FOR YOU.

ROUND FOUR: RETRIEVE THIS POSTCARD
WHILE STANDING ON ONE LEG.

ROUND FIVE: RETRIEVE THIS POSTCARD
USING A TOOL OR UTENSIL.

PLACE
STAMP
HERE

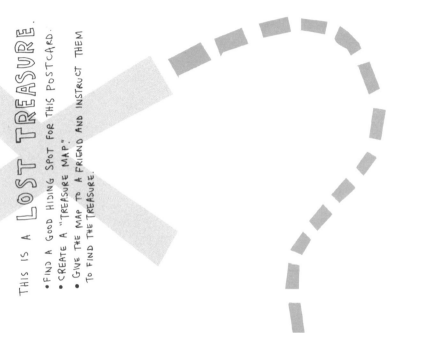

THIS IS A LOST TREASURE.

- FIND A GOOD HIDING SPOT FOR THIS POSTCARD.
- CREATE A "TREASURE MAP".
- GIVE THE MAP TO A FRIEND AND INSTRUCT THEM TO FIND THE TREASURE.

PLACE
STAMP
HERE

EXPERIENCE MAP

MAP PLACES ASSOCIATED
WITH YOUR MEMORIES.

HAND MAP

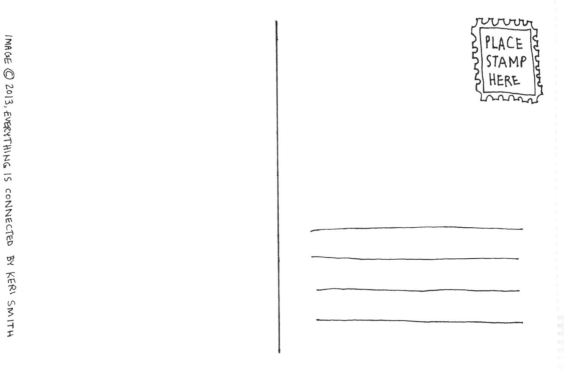

PLACE
STAMP
HERE

DETAILED EVENTS OF A
DAY IN THE FUTURE.

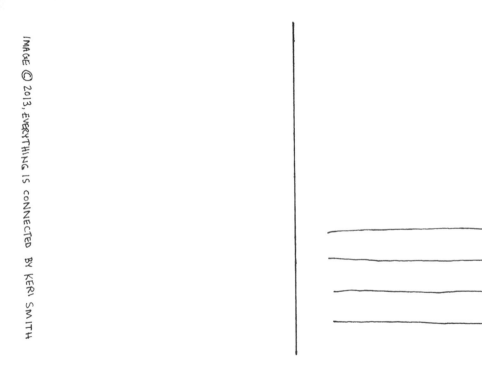

PLACE
STAMP
HERE

POST CARD
OF RANDOM
THOUGHTS.

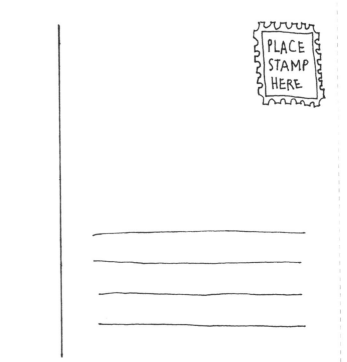

PLACE
STAMP
HERE

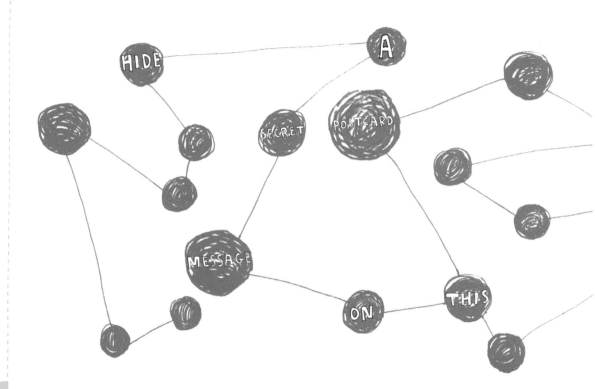

PLACE
STAMP
HERE

THIS POSTCARD IS A SIGN.
WHAT DO YOU WANT IT TO SAY?

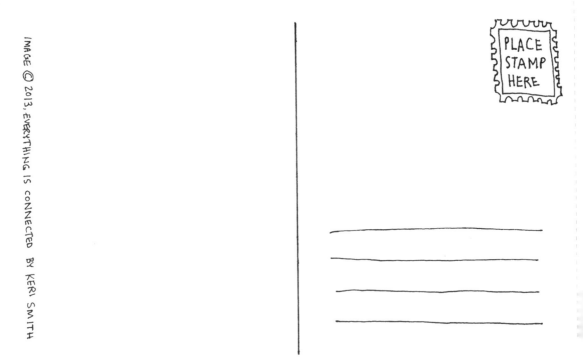

PLACE
STAMP
HERE

FORTUNE TELLER
• CUT OUT SQUARES.
• ASK A YES OR NO QUESTION.
• CLOSE EYES AND PICK A
  SQUARE FOR YOUR ANSWER.

YES

MAYBE

NO

TRY
AGAIN

THIS IS A
MYSTERY

PLACE
STAMP
HERE

IDEA FORMULATION GENERATOR

- IN BOX ONE MAKE A LIST OF THINGS FOUND IN NATURE.

- IN BOX TWO MAKE A LIST OF OBJECTS YOU USE EVERY DAY.

- IN BOX THREE MAKE A LIST OF WORDS YOU LIKE.

- PICK ONE ITEM FROM EACH LIST AND COMBINE THEM TO COME UP WITH AN IDEA FOR A NEW PRODUCT OR CONCEPT.

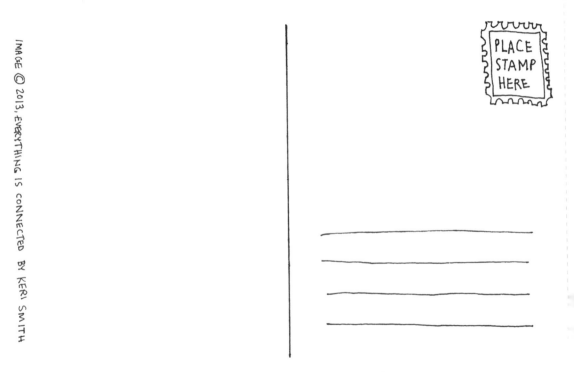

PLACE
STAMP
HERE

ACTION POSTCARD

COME UP WITH AN
INTERESTING WAY TO
MAKE THIS CARD MOVE.

PLACE
STAMP
HERE

RANDOM LETTER

Get a dictionary.
• The first word of your letter must be chosen from page 48.
• The fifth word of your letter must be chosen from page 10.
• The twelfth word of your letter must be chosen from page 100.
• The eighteenth word of your letter must be chosen from page 25.

PLACE
STAMP
HERE

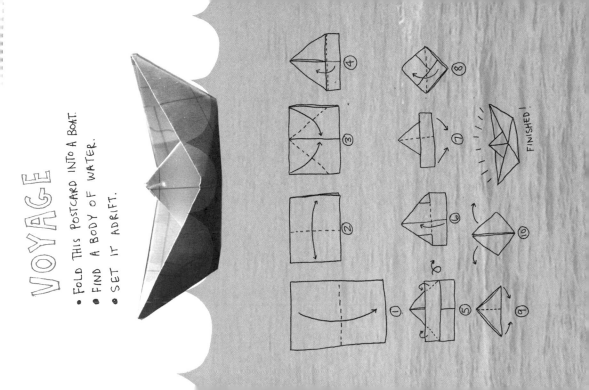

VOYAGE

- FOLD THIS POSTCARD INTO A BOAT.
- FIND A BODY OF WATER.
- SET IT ADRIFT.

① ② ③ ④
⑤ ⑥ ⑦ ⑧
⑨ ⑩

FINISHED!

PLACE
STAMP
HERE

SMUDGE LOG

Create random smudges in each of these squares while you are going about your day.

- Experiment with different substances.
- Document where and when each smudge was made.

DATE	DATE	DATE
TIME	TIME	TIME
LOCATION	LOCATION	LOCATION
DATE	DATE	DATE
TIME	TIME	TIME
LOCATION	LOCATION	LOCATION
DATE	DATE	DATE
TIME	TIME	TIME
LOCATION	LOCATION	LOCATION
DATE	DATE	DATE
TIME	TIME	TIME
LOCATION	LOCATION	LOCATION

PLACE
STAMP
HERE

PLACE
STAMP
HERE

PLACE
STAMP
HERE

USE THIS POSTCARD
TO COVER UP OR
REPLACE SOMETHING
YOU DON'T LIKE ON
A BULLETIN BOARD.

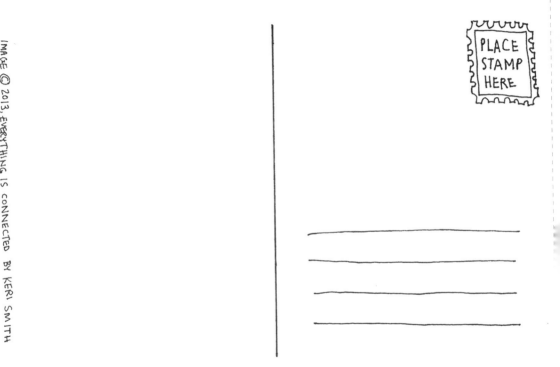

PLACE
STAMP
HERE

TIME TRAVEL DEVICE

- THINK OF A TIME AND PLACE YOU WOULD LIKE TO REVISIT. ENTER IT ON THE SCREEN BELOW.

- MAKE DETAILED NOTES INCLUDING EVERYTHING YOU CAN REMEMBER ABOUT THAT TIME—COLORS, SMELLS, LIGHT, TIME OF DAY, NAMES, SPACE.

- ALTERNATE: WRITE ABOUT A FUTURE TIME AND PLACE USING YOUR IMAGINATION.

PLACE
STAMP
HERE

SEND THIS POSTCARD TO
SOMEONE WITH THE SAME
NAME AS YOU.

KERI SMITH
LOCATION: SOUTHERN CALIFORNIA
WORKS AT LOMA LINDA UNIVERSITY
INFO: ADMISSIONS OFFICER SCHOOL OF
DENTISTRY

KERI SMITH
LOCATION: KENNETT, MISSOURI
INFO: NEW BRANCH MANAGER
OF AMERICAN HOMECARE DATE: FEB 17, 2007

KERI SMITH
LOCATION: UNKNOWN
INFO: WORKS FOR
BCAA TRAVEL

KERI SMITH
LOCATION: CHELAN, WASHINGTON
DATE: JULY 21, 2003
INFO: HAS A LARGE FAMILY &
LOTS OF KIDS. GOES ON YEARLY
VACATIONS.

KERI SMITH
LOCATION: OKLAHOMA
UNIVERSITY
INFO: CHEERLEADER
DATE: 2006

KERI SMITH
LOCATION: CHARLOTTE, NC
INFO: STUDENT ASSIST.
UNIVERSITY OF NC

PLACE
STAMP
HERE

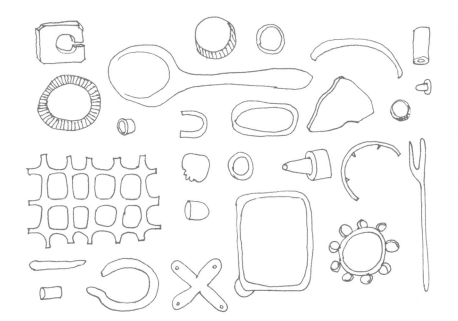

SEND A SMALL COLLECTION OF FOUND FLAT THINGS TO A FRIEND. FIGURE OUT A WAY TO ATTACH THEM TO THIS POSTCARD, OR USE AN ENVELOPE. ASK THEM TO DO SOMETHING WITH THE COLLECTION AND SEND IT BACK TO YOU.

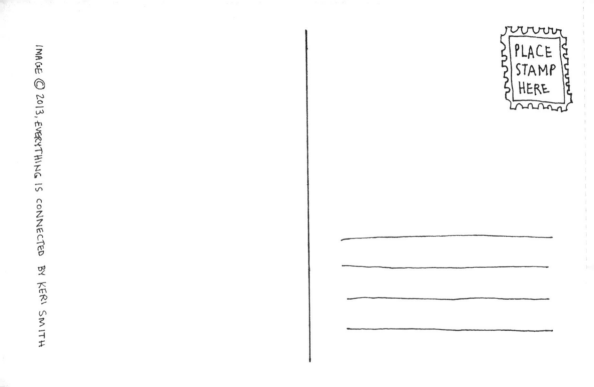

PLACE
STAMP
HERE

CURRENCY

USE THIS MONEY TO BEGIN YOUR
OWN ECONOMY AND BARTER SYSTEM.

TRADE THIS POSTCARD FOR ANOTHER ITEM
OF EQUAL OR GREATER VALUE.

PLACE A PHOTO
OF YOURSELF HERE

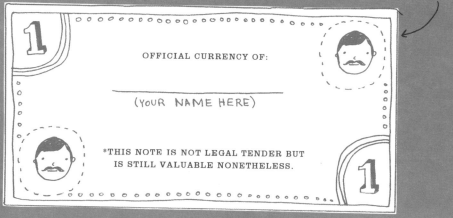

1

OFFICIAL CURRENCY OF:

_____

(YOUR NAME HERE)

*THIS NOTE IS NOT LEGAL TENDER BUT
IS STILL VALUABLE NONETHELESS.

1

PLACE
STAMP
HERE

THE FOREST

THIS IS A FOREST TO GET LOST IN. YOU MIGHT WANT TO THINK OF IT AS A MINI-RETREAT, OR A PLACE TO SIT AND THINK. YOU MIGHT WANT TO DREAM ABOUT BUILDING A CABIN HERE, OR JUST IMAGINE TAKING A WALK WITH SOMEONE YOU LOVE. ENJOY THE SMELLS AND THE FEELING OF YOUR FEET ON THE EARTH. OH, THE SUN JUST CAME OUT! WHAT SOUNDS CAN YOU HEAR NOW?

PLACE
STAMP
HERE